Socialism And Economic Cybernetics

– *Towards a Manifesto*

Elena Veduta

**Head of the Department of
Strategic Planning and Economic Policy,
Lomonosov Moscow State University.**

Copyright © Elena Veduta 2024

All Rights Reserved

All rights reserved. No part of this publication may be reproduced, distributed, or transmitted in any form or by any means, including photocopying, recording, or other electronic or mechanical methods, without the author's prior written permission, except in the case of brief quotations embodied in critical reviews and certain other non-commercial uses permitted by copyright law. For permission requests, please get in touch with the author.

Publisher:

Second Wave Publications,

B M Box 2978,

London,

WC1N 3XX,

UK.

secondwave@hotmail.co.uk

Designed and printed by Amazon

Cover Design: Eswari K (Fiverr)

Published in February 2024

Author can be contacted as follows:

Dr. Elena Veduta.

veduta@list.ru

Contents

Dedication i

Acknowledgements ii

About the Author iii

Publisher's Notes vi

Abstract vii

Introduction 1

Chapter I The End of Capitalist History 5

Chapter II The Project of the Socialist Economy: "USSR" 12

Chapter III Digital Projects of the Capitalist and Socialist Economy 28

Conclusions 42

References 48

Appendix 55

Dedication

Dedicated to the memory of thousands of comrades around the world who gave their lives in the fight to free humanity from class exploitation.

Acknowledgements

Second Wave Publications is immensely grateful to the author, Professor Elena Veduta, for granting us the privilege of publishing this work.

With due respect we acknowledge previous publications of the full text of this work in Russian Federation as well as a part of it, by the American journal Monthly Review (volume74, Number5, October 2022).

We would like to extend our warmest regards to our longstanding colleagues Wilf Dixon and Peter Tobin, for their invaluable assistance and cooperation with the editing of this text.

Last but not the least we would like to express our sincere gratitude for Helen Cooper and the other members of the Amazon Book Editorial Department, whose expertise, insights, and encouragement made it possible for us to complete this work.

About the Author

Elena Veduta, a celebrated cybernetic economist and active participant in political movements in Russia and abroad, was born in Kharkiv, Ukraine.

Theoretical achievements

Her outstanding theoretical expertise is rooted in her remarkable academic journey, which began in 1967, when she graduated with a gold medal in Physics and Mathematics from Minsk, Belarus.

Studying at the Faculty of Economics of the Lomonosov Moscow State University from 1968 till 1973 she graduated with honours in "Economic Cybernetics. This was followed by a successful defence of a Ph.D. thesis, studying at the Department of Mathematical Methods of Economic Analysis of the same university from 1973 till 1976.

She then worked for nearly two decades at the Department of National Economy Planning of Plekhanov Russian University of Economics.

In 1999, she received her unique Russian doctorate in economics. Two years later, in 2001, she was awarded the title of Professor.

Since 2003, Prof. Veduta has been working at the Lomonosov Moscow State University, and since 2014 she has been the Head of its Department of Strategic Planning and Economic Policy.

Scientific publications and institutional engagements

Professor Elena Veduta's unique research on Marxist political economy, strategic planning and economic policy, economic security and economic cybernetics has resulted in more than 90 scientific articles and several influential monographs. These include: "State Economic Strategies" (1998), Strategy and Economic Policy of the State (2003) and "Intersectoral - Interbranch Balance: The Mechanism of Strategic Planning of the Economy" (2016).

For scientific activity Professor Veduta was awarded the title of academician of the International Academy of Management, head of the section "Artificial Intelligence in Economics" of the Scientific Council of the Russian Academy of Sciences on the Methodology of Artificial Intelligence and Cognitive Research, member of the Academic Council of N Baibakov International Public Foundation for the Promotion of Economic Development and member of the editorial board of the journal "Digital Economy", published by the Central Economics and Mathematics Institute of the Russian Academy of Sciences.

Political participation

Elena Veduta is a true Marxist, striving to bring knowledge to people and put it into practice.

She voluntarily worked as an aide Deputy in the State Duma of the Russian Federation to General Valentin

Varennikov, a member of the State Emergency Committee established in 1991 to avert the collapse of the USSR. She has continued to take part in State Duma proceedings as a specialist on the approval of the law on strategic planning and at the Military-Industrial Complex's commission on Economics and Mathematical modelling.

Trying to spread the knowledge of Marxism and economic cybernetics among the population, she speaks a lot in mass media. She gave many lectures in the news agencies (NA) "Aurora", "Icebreaker" of Mark Sorkin, "School of Common Sense", "Regnum", "Red Spring". She regularly acts as an expert in NA "Aurora", "Interception of Management", "Public News Service", RBC TV (RosBusinessConsulting), Tsargrad, Public Television of Russia, and the First Channel of Television.

On the global arena, Elena Veduta is a Member of the Scientific Council of the International Forum, "Bandung Spirit".

Publisher's Notes

The author of this work, Dr. Elena Veduta, has felt it necessary to call attention to the critical significance of economic cybernetics for socialist economic planning during the Second Industrial Revolution. This, in fact, originated in the work of her late father, Prof. Nikolay Veduta, in response to the historic sabotage of the USSR by reactionary academic economists of the school of so-called 'commodity socialism' in the middle of the 1950s and the ever-expanding privileged nomenklatura. Through her extensive writing on the subject, she has brought it to a historically unprecedented and urgently necessary level in Marxist economic theory and practice.

Political activists and theorists have been introduced to the growing, distinctive function of economic cybernetics for socialism before, but never by someone whose mastery of the subject is as exceptional as her unrivalled authenticity thanks to her close ties to former Soviet society and her research experiences at numerous eminent Russian Federation organizations.

This brief manifesto poses a challenging query to those who identify themselves as Marxists: Are we strategically prepared to meet the challenges of the twenty-first century?

We welcome socialists from all around the world to participate in a discussion about what the international socialist movement's program should be for the new period.

Kumar Sarkar,
Coordinator,
Second Wave Publications,
London.

Abstract

The concentration and centralisation of capital, which began after the first industrial revolution in the late 18th century, led in the early 20th century to the dominance of transnational corporations (TNCs), which launched the First and Second World Wars and the Cold War with the USSR. After the collapse of the USSR in 1991, the world became unipolar, dominated by TNCs, which used monetary instruments, institutional reforms, colour revolutions, and military actions to redistribute the generated incomes and assets of all states in their favour. A contribution was made by post-pandemic digital transformation in 2020, aimed at using the achievements of the digital revolution to establish their global digital governance of people in order to preserve the capitalist economy. This article argues that within the framework of the capitalist economy, where all is guided by profit maximisation, as evidenced by historical experience hitherto, it is impossible for civilisation to get out of the global crisis. Using old tools and digital technologies to manage people does not eliminate the main cause of the global crisis – i.e., disproportionate economic development. The only project aimed at solving economic problems by planning the national economy was the project of the USSR.

The use of the method of successive approximations (iterations) with feedback in the planning of the economy allowed the USSR to become one pole in the post-war bipolar world. However, the departure of the Party (2) nomenklatura from Marxism, democracy, and its preference for manual control over automisation determined the USSR's defeat in the Cold War. It proved the need to use in state (global) management an economic robot based on cybernetic planning of the interaction of all industries and sectors of the economy in order for civilisation to enter a trajectory of growth in the quality of life and the cultural development of the individual personality.

Introduction

The relevance of current research

Since the beginning of 2020, the world has been experiencing a series of intensifying crises. The rapidly growing threats of the global crisis are forcing transnational corporations (TNCs) and governments of all countries to initiate new development projects and anti-crisis measures.

The main ideologist of modern capitalism, the World Economic Forum (WEF) in Davos, held in 2021, it was noted that, due to the pandemic, global coordination in the form of trade (market economy) began to carry high risks of a recession in the world economy associated with the rupture of inter-sectoral and inter-state economic ties, loss of working time, and rising world prices. To reduce these risks in global value chains, it was recommended that "closer to home" alternatives be sought.

Again, in January 2023, the WEF demonstrated total helplessness in developing a plan to save the economy from recession, replacing its discussion with the approval of increasing arms support for Ukraine. In fact, the forum once again confirmed that the current command-administrative system of global governance in the form of market economy only increases the risks, thus bringing the catastrophe closer.

Alternative to the market economy is the cybernetic economy, based on the cybernetic planning of the national (inter-state) economy, ensuring the proportional development of the economy for the exit of civilisation on the highway of social progress and the cultural development of the individual.

Scientific new thinking

The main reason for the global crisis is a global system of governance in the form of market economy that is unable to ensure the proportional development of the economy in the direction of an increase in the quality of life. It has been proved, for the first time, that this reason cannot be overcome by financial methods of regulating the capitalist economy or by manual planning of a socialist economy. It requires a transition to the cybernetic economy – automisation of economic management (the use of an economic robot, AI in the economy) based on cybernetic planning as a system of algorithms for coordinating the orders of end-users with the capabilities of manufacturers. Such a system of algorithms is a 'dynamic model of the intersectoral balance' (MIB).

The objective of this article is to prove the need for a transition to a socialist economy in the form of cybernetic economy using cybernetic planning of the economy for civilisation to enter the mainstream of social progress and the cultural development of the individual.

To reach this goal, the *following tasks* are necessary:

- to substantiate the impossibility of overcoming the current global crisis within the framework of the capitalist economy;
- using the principle of historicism, study the experience of planning the socialist economy of the USSR, which made the USSR a country that determined the development trends of the bipolar world, and identify the reasons for the USSR's abandonment of the socialist economy;
- show the futility of using the achievements of the digital revolution to get the capitalist economy out of the global crisis;
- to substantiate the necessity of introducing an cybernetic economy (economic robot or AI in economy) based on the cybernetic planning of a socialist economy in order for civilisation to continue on the highway of future prosperity.

The purpose and tasks of the article determine its structure.

The *first section* examines the historical experience of regulating the capitalist economy and proves the impossibility of overcoming the current global crisis using financial, institutional, and other tools from the arsenal of capitalism.

The *second section* examines an alternative experience in coordinating production relationships in the form of planning the USSR's economy. The reasons for its success and failure are investigated using the principle of historicism.

The *third section* proves the hopelessness of the digitalisation of the capitalist economy. The necessity of the transition to a socialist economy with the use of an cybernetic economy based on a dynamic model of input-output balance is substantiated in order to drive the highway to a prosperous future.

Chapter I
The End of Capitalist History

The strategy and economic policy of capitalism are based on the generalisation of more than a thousand years of experience in the trade of goods and money, the exploitation of labour, and the use of cheap resources of dependent countries. By the 20th century, the economic policy of capitalist states was characterised by the cyclical nature of "mercantilism – war – liberalism" (Veduta, 2019). **(1)**

Mercantilism is characterised by state intervention in the economy on the principles of protectionism, indicative planning in the interests of the dominant social strata, and colonial policy to provide the leading countries with cheap raw materials and labour, sales markets of dependent countries. History from the 17th to the 20th century confirms the gravitation of mercantilism toward the use of armed force to protect the interests of competing metropolises.

The first industrial revolution, which began at the end of the 18th century, was marked by the emergence of machines that operated several mechanical tools at once, overcoming the physical limitations of humans. Machines became the basis for an unprecedented increase in labour productivity (Marx, 1951). **(2)** Its result was the establishment in the 19th century of the capitalist mode of production, aimed at maximising the profits of the capitalists through unequal exchange with hired labour and with dependent countries.

The politics of mercantilism and the transition to capitalism ended in the Napoleonic wars. A Liberal government came to power in 1822 in England, which had become the dominant industrial and financial power. It became profitable to abandon protectionism in favour of liberalism, which advocated the idea of free trade in order to realise England's competitive advantages. Periodically occurring economic crises resulted from the spontaneous (disproportionate) development of the capitalist economy. The Central Bank became the regulator of the economy, which supported the free convertibility of banknotes for gold with a discount policy (Veduta, 2023). **(3)** At that time, most entrepreneurs were not interested in inflation since profits, in the conditions of developing the world market and reducing production costs, were high due to machines.

During crises, when the interest rate reaches its maximum and the stock price, on the contrary, reaches its minimum, there is a rapid centralisation of capital when larger capital buys up smaller capital. Each crisis means a renewal of the production base, an increase in unemployment, social and technological inequality between countries, and the centralisation of capital. As a result of the crisis development of capitalism, free competition, which seemed to be the ideal economic mechanism to ensure the dictate of the consumers over the producers and the renewal of the production base, was gradually replaced by the dominance of corporations.

The ideas of the independence of the Central Bank and the monetary system in the form of a gold standard were used by England to create in Paris in 1867 the first 'international monetary system' (IMS). This allowed Britain to have a growing trade deficit, which meant the launch of global inflation, redistributing incomes and assets in favour of 'transnational corporations (TNCs) based in Britain.

In the last third of the 19th century, the world became multipolar again. Germany, the USA, Japan, and Italy began to threaten British superiority. These states, contributing to the emergence of capitalist corporations in them, began to pursue a protectionist policy of neo-mercantilism based on the principles of free enterprises, protectionist tariffs, and colonial expansion. The struggle of states for markets in the interests of capitalist corporations became more violent.

By the early 20th century, the authority of the TNCs had been established. They had imposed their global project on the world community, launching general world inflation to redistribute the incomes and assets of all other social strata of the world in their favour. Since the First World War, which brought down all international agreements on the IMS based on the gold standard (Pesenti,1976) **(4)**, TNCs have implemented a global project of interfering with the monetary policy of central banks. The cyclical nature of the economic policy of states in the phases of the cycle "mercantilism-war-liberalism ..." was transformed into the cyclical nature of "inflation-war-financial stabilisation...".

Inflation is becoming general and chronic. On the eve of war, during it, and after, rapid inflation was used to restore the economy. In the period between the wars, financial stabilisation was used, and a new IMS was created, based on gold and key reserve currencies of the West for their export to dependent countries in exchange for the goods produced by them. So, in the last century, after the policy of financial stabilisation (liberalism) in Europe in the 1920s, there was a transition to inflation in the 1930s. When the USA and Great Britain used protectionism to contain inflation, Germany and the USSR saw rapid inflation with the creation of a centralised system of economic management aimed at military needs (mobilisation models). This period, accompanied by a "war" of trade duties and currency devaluations, ended with World War II. World wars, providing a forcible exit of society from the global crisis, are becoming more and more destructive for humanity (Marx, 1951) **(5)**.

After World War II, the IMS was created on the basis of the gold dollar standard. Thanks to the creation by TNCs in 1958 of the world market for loan capital, whose operations are free from state regulation, and its development, gold was gradually replaced by the end of the 1960s as the basis for determining currency parities. After the 1973–1975 economic crisis, the Jamaican monetary system was established based on the US dollar and controlled by the IMF, allowing an endless deficit build-up in the US balance of payments in the interests of TNCs. The global loan capital market created by the TNCs in 1958 allows fictitious capital to be exported to other countries, which increases technological and social inequality in the world. Sooner or later, speculative games will end with protectionism and preparations for another military solution to the crisis.

The coordinated financial policy of Western countries to integrate their national financial markets into the global loan capital market was completed by 1991, when the USSR lost the Cold War and collapsed. The flows of fictitious capital from the West were directed towards the "division" of the property of the former USSR and the countries of Eastern Europe. The former republics of the USSR began to pursue a policy of financial stabilisation under the banner of liberalisation. The unipolar world established in 1991 is globally governed by TNCs.

At the same time, the growth of economic chaos and the redistribution of income and assets in favour of TNCs are achieved through the use of monetary instruments, reforms, colour revolutions, the military, and other actions. The theoretical justification for this lawlessness is a mixture of analytical economic and political theories, inconsistent accounting information, the international standard for national accounting with a huge re-count, the balance of payments, which equates production and fictitious investment, and predictive scenarios of development obtained on the basis of econometric models, which are a mixture of mathematics and statistics to quantify economic phenomena, not related to the real course of events.

Following the usual "rules" of the global capitalist project, the United States, with the coming to power of Trump in 2017, began scrapping liberalism for the transition to protectionism. The world has entered another phase of pre-war protectionism.

Considering the nuclear potential of developing countries and therefore trying to avoid direct military conflict, the TNCs added the achievements of the digital revolution to their tools, in particular for the creation of artificial intelligence (AI) and for organising cyber-attacks and cyber warfare, destabilising computer systems and life in states seeking national information security. (The White House, 2018) **(6)**.

The pandemic-2019 has revealed to almost everyone the goals of TNCs seeking to use the opportunities presented by the digital revolution to preserve capitalism by establishing total control over human behaviour. Since the beginning of

2020, the world has been going through alternating accelerated and intensifying crises.

To solve the crisis problems, the West provoked the Special Military Operation (SMO) of Russia against Ukraine. It is gradually developing its assistance in Ukraine, dragging out the SMO as long as possible in order to justify the widespread deterioration in living standards in all countries, including the West. By dragging nuclear Russia into the SMO, the West is increasing the production of military equipment and is trying to economically destroy its main competitor in the Third World War, which it organised.

The main ideologist of modern capitalism, the World Economic Forum in Davos, held in January 2023, demonstrated total helplessness in developing plans to save the economy from recession. The forum discussed not economic problems but the build-up of armaments for Ukraine. Thus, the forum confirmed that the current command and the control system of global governance only increases the risk of World War III and the transition to a mobilisation model of total control of people with the help of artificial intelligence (AI) and biotechnologies, thereby bringing the end of human history closer.

Chapter II
The Project of the Socialist Economy: "USSR"

Socialism is the only alternative to all capitalist global projects that ensure the cultural progress of mankind.

The first attempt in the world to create a socialist, proportionally developing economy in the direction of increasing the quality of life was made in the USSR. The USSR managed to turn itself into an industrial power that defeated fascism in World War II and then became one of the poles of the bipolar world. However, in the Cold War, the socialist economy of the USSR lost to the capitalist superpower United States, and capitalism returned to Russia. Therefore, an analysis of the planned economy as experienced in the USSR, its mistakes, subversions, and their causes is extremely relevant for the implementation of a new socialist project of a socialist economy, which will finally overthrow capitalism.

Marx linked revolutionary changes in the system of social production with the emergence of tools of labour that sharply increased labour productivity. Therefore, the question naturally arises: What instrument of labour should serve as the material and technical basis for the second industrial revolution, which will forever change the capitalist system to a socialist one? Marx did not answer this question, but it is known that he was against the socialist revolution in backward Russia. In his opinion, "Russia does not need either a European-style revolution or the Western path of development because the matter will inevitably turn into the forcible submission of a multimillion population to the inexorable laws of capitalism with a tragic ending - the irreversible degradation of the entire nation" (Lutsenko A., 2018, p.117) **(7)**. However, he did not say in his research anything about the instrument of labour that would significantly increase the growth of labour productivity and lead to socialism.

Who was right: Marx, who warned of the tragic finale of the revolution in a backward country, or Lenin, who carried out a socialist revolution in a backward Russia?

On the one hand, the successes achieved by the USSR, thanks to the socialist revolution of 1917, in transforming a backward agrarian and raw-material-rich country with a huge foreign debt into an advanced scientific and technological power that determined a bipolar world are awesome. On the other hand, after the counter-revolution of 1991, Russia "returned" to its past. It has again become a raw-material appendage of the world capitalist community and continues to "slide" downward.

Depending on the emerging conditions and the accumulation of experience in planning the economy, the model of the socialist economy in the USSR changed. In its construction, the following periods can be distinguished: war communism, the new economic policy (NEP), the course of industrialisation and the dismantling of economic planning.

A) War Communism (1918-1921)

The Great October Socialist Revolution of 1917 established the power of the Soviets of Workers', Soldiers' and Peasants' Deputies in Russia by March 1918. The Soviet state developed the first food balances for the survival of people and, at the same time, proceeded to construct the future in the interests of the people. In its initial years, during an extremely difficult anarchic situation, when chaos reigned, there was a civil war and a war against the intervention of many Entente countries. Soviet Russia, under the leadership of Lenin, managed to maintain power in the country and did not allow it to collapse into pieces. Solving then the most difficult task of retaining power, Lenin, at the same time, was engaged in the most advanced direction of technical progress as conceived by him - the electrification of the whole country.

The country introduced a monopoly on foreign trade and foreign currency transactions, nationalised land, industrial enterprises, transport and banks, banned private trade of essential products, introduced general labour conscription, workers control over the production and distribution of vital products. The Supreme Council of the National Economy was responsible for coordinating the activities of enterprises to implement quarterly and then, later, annual plans (Veduta, 2023 **(3)**).

In 1920, the country adopted the strategic plan GOELRO ("State Commission for the Electrification of Russia"). It considered electrification as a "powerful factor" in the growth of labour productivity. The GOELRO was based on an analysis of social needs and their balancing with available resources (input-output) with reference to territorial development plans. It was designed for 10-15 years to restore the economy to the pre-war level. In 1921, for its implementation, the State Planning Committee (GOSPLAN / Gosudarstvennyy Planovyy Komitet) was created to develop a national economic plan based on the electrification project and for general monitoring of the implementation of this plan (Administration of the affairs of the Council of People's Commissars of the USSR,1944) **(8)**.

Implementation of the GOELRO was faced with great difficulties. Knowledge about the current state of affairs and ensuring the balanced development of the economy was insufficient. Scheduling errors led to increased imbalances, production shutdowns, and plant closures. The country was thus forced to switch to the New Economic Policy (NEP).

B) NEP (1921-1927)

It seemed that NEP, based on a mixed economy with different forms of ownership and preserving the state's commanding heights in the economy, was a step backwards. However, it was a necessary one for the practical construction of socialism, requiring an understanding of the importance of using different forms of property since the Soviet state, still in its infancy, was not able to manage everything effectively. The principle of 'party maximum' was introduced in June 1921 for party members who were leading employees of institutions and enterprises. The idea came from the Paris Commune of 1871. According to it, the salary of responsible employees should not exceed 150% of the average salary in the enterprises under their control. (Site: The enemy of capital, 2015) **(9)**.

The goal of the NEP was to restore the national economy by maintaining control over heavy industry, transport, banks, wholesale and international trade, introducing private entrepreneurship and raising foreign capital. State-owned enterprises competed with each other. Agriculture, retail trade, services, food, and light industries were mostly in private hands.

GOSPLAN began to develop the most important balance sheets for fodder for livestock, sugar, rubber, metal, etc. The balances developed by the GOSPLAN for 1924 were brought together in a single table - the balance of the national economy, covering the most important inter-sectoral product flows. In the introduction to this work, P. Popov wrote that.

"... neither in the statistical, nor in the economic literature, nor in the Russian, nor in the Western European literature, were there examples of such works, and we had to decide on our own in the process of the work, not only on the technical method of research, but also the methodological prerequisites"(Elimeev, 1999, p. 35 **(10)**

This balance was developed in the 30s in the USA by V. Leontiev, using the apparatus of linear algebra to build an economic-mathematical model "input-output" for the analysis of the structure of the American economy.

The Balance was criticised by Stalin, who called it "a game of numbers" (Stalin, 1929) **(11)**. It is believed by some that Stalin's negative reaction to this work was because the balance contradicted the policy of forced industrialisation, which broke all the existing proportions in the economy. However, the reason was different. Stalin, as the manager of the development of a huge country, was interested in algorithms for solving strategic problems and not just a "picture".

In 1926, the national economy was restored to the level of 1913. Then began a slowdown in economic growth and an increase in unemployment. The "price scissors" between monopoly high prices for industrial products and low prices for agricultural products reached a level that the village refused to trade with the city. Therefore, a famine appeared in the city. Faced with growing economic problems, the Bolsheviks began a discussion in 1926-1928 about a planning model capable of ensuring a high rate of industrialisation (Koen,1988) **(12)**.

The rightists (N. Bukharin, V. Bazarov, N. Kondratyev) believed that the market would decide for itself, the state should only correct the negative consequences through forecasts. The leftists (G. Krzhizhanovsky, V. Kuibyshev, S. Strumilin) opposed this position. They wanted to manage the economy to solve the country's tasks for its accelerated industrialisation (Autonomov, 2000) **(13)**. They put forward the brilliant idea of drawing up a plan by the method of successive approximations (iterations), which would coordinate government orders with production capabilities. It was the idea of living cybernetic planning of the economy, with feedback from manufacturers, and with adjustments to government orders depending on the ability of manufacturers.

C) The course of industrialisation, war and economic recovery (1928-1950)

The government of the USSR made the transition from the NEP to the course of industrialisation at the end of the 1920s. The core of the course was the perspective for 5 years of planning of the economy with the coordination of planned input-output calculations at all levels of the management hierarchy by the method of iterations to achieve goals in the sliding (live) planning mode. Investments became a managerial parameters of the plan.

The starting points for planning were government orders to ensure the priority development of key industries and the planned fund for public working time. Further, material, labour and financial resources were calculated by building the necessary production chains for determining capital investments to create additional manufacturing capacities. After all intra-sectoral calculations were carried out, applications for the material, labour and financial resources were supplied to the top coordinating body - GOSPLAN. After considering the real capabilities of manufacturers, the assignments for state orders were corrected, and a new calculation of the plan began. The calculations continued until a balanced input-output plan was obtained within the specified calculation accuracy. Only after that were contracts concluded between the enterprises, and the plan turned into a directive. Since the economic situation could change, the principle of rolling planning was applied to timely adjust the previously drawn-up plan in a timely manner. (Online).

During 1929 - June 1934, the USSR took 1st place in Europe and 2nd in the world in terms of industrial production and national income (Barr R.,1995) **(14)**.

The highest mobilisation qualities were demonstrated by the planned economy of the USSR during the Second World War. Quarterly, monthly and ten-day plans became the main form of planning. Although smelting about 3 times less steel and producing almost 5 times less coal than Germany, the USSR created almost twice as many weapons and military equipment during the war. (Veduta, 2023) **(3)**.

After the war, the course towards the industrialisation of the economy in the USSR continued. From 1947-1954, every year, the real incomes of the population increased by 34% against the pre-war level. The gold content of the rouble had been established in 1950.

Competition between the United States and the USSR began in the conditions of the Cold War. US strategy became the export of investments to other countries with the construction of a unipolar world at the expense of the dollar-based IMF. The strategy of the USSR remained in the course of industrialisation at the expense of the national economy.

It should be noted that Stalin paid great attention to the development of artel (cooperative) activities based on collective ownership of the means of production in the absence of hired workers and the activities of single handicraftsmen. Artels received their legal right to exist in

1936 with the adoption of a new constitution in the Soviet Union. Artel could not be bought, sold, inherited, etc.; all its property was the equal collective property of the employees of the enterprise, the right to use of which was cancelled upon leaving the artel. Artels participated in a variety of areas - from the food industry to metalworking and from jewellery to the chemical industry. In the early 1940s, the artels were forbidden by the authorities to interfere in their activities unless the law was violated. The main requirement of the state was the proximity of retail prices for the same goods in cooperatives and state enterprises. The country's leadership created conditions for limiting corruption in artels. State-owned enterprises did not provide benefits to artels.

At the time of the death of Joseph Stalin in the USSR, there were 114,000 artels and lone handicraftsmen employing about two million people, who produced almost 6% of the gross industrial output of the USSR. In 1955, the productivity of labour in the system of artels grew almost 2.5 times in comparison with 1940. (Logvinov, 2021) **(15)**

In the "clash" of the superpowers, there were unequal starting conditions. During the war, US industry doubled, and US gold reserves accounted for more than 70% of the world's gold reserves (Veduta, 2023) **(3)**. The main achievement of the United States was the emergence of the science of cybernetics, which studied information processes for the creation of automated control systems (ACS). After the economic recovery, the USSR's leadership should have seen the importance of cybernetics in the development of economic planning. Instead, this new science was incorrectly described as a pseudoscience, which slowed down its development in the USSR by almost 10 years.

D) The collapse of the project of the socialist economy of the USSR (1950-1991)

Supporting military parity with the United States was not enough to enable the USSR to win the Cold War. *The continuation of the hitherto course of industrialisation after the war meant a disproportionate development of the economy, inevitably leading to an economic crisis. The USSR needed a transition from the priority development of industries that determined technological progress to a path of the model of proportional development of the economy in the direction of growth of the quality of life.*

Khrushchev, having come to power after Stalin's death, "buried" the artel movement in the USSR. He destroyed artels because his party, nomenklatura, did not like the fact that many skilled and talented people who left factories for artels earned more than factory directors and party workers. On April 14, 1956, a resolution of the Central Committee of the CPSU and the Council of Ministers of the USSR - "On the reorganisation of commercial cooperation"- appeared, according to which artel enterprises were transferred to the state. The property of enterprises was alienated free of charge. In the end, all artels by the 1960s became state property. An exception was made only for small household producers; then, they were forbidden to independently carry out regular retail trade. The few surviving artels were limited in their activities. To sell their products, they had to obtain special state permits and sell only on collective farm markets.

One of the worst manifestations of this pogrom was the despicable Soviet deficit. Under Stalin, when tens of thousands of artel-cooperatives and hundreds of thousands of single handicraftsmen operated in the country, the needs for food of the people were satisfied by collective farm markets, individual peasants and collective farmers with personal plots; there was no such problem. In the Stalinist USSR, the problem of a shortage of any product (usually food or household goods, that is what artels specialised in) was solved at the local level.

By the 1950s, the economy of the USSR was faced with the problem of processing a colossal amount of information for planning the national economy. The volume of production increased, and production relationships became more complex, which required many iterations to draw up the plan. This was not possible with manual planning. It required the automatisation of state management of the economy and the development of artels and lone handicraftsmen in industries directly related to meeting the needs of households.

Disregard for cybernetics drew the country into discussions about the economic problems of socialism, which continued after Stalin's death and was followed by the imposition of a damaging theory of commodity production under socialism, which served to degradation of the economy of the USSR by initiating economic chaos and eventually restoring capitalism in 1991.

The complex manual control of a huge country required automation. After a discussion that took place in 1956-1957 at the Institute of Economics (Moscow) under the leadership of Academician K. Ostrovityanov, the aforementioned incorrect theory of 'commodity production under socialism' was officially adopted. It completely contradicted the teachings of Marx regarding socialism and the practice of economic planning. According to it, on the one hand, state-owned enterprises work according to the plan and, on the other hand, for profit.

This perverted doctrine divided the country's economists into two camps: Marxists, who denied the commodity nature of production under socialism (the so-called no-commodity supporters), and the restorers of capitalism, who wished to promote it (the so-called commodity supporters). The ideological struggle between economists received a new impetus with the awareness of the need to use cybernetics to solve economic problems.

While cyberneticists were busy solving the most complex problem of automatisation economic management, Party nomenklatura, afraid of losing privileges of manual control, stubbornly imposed the implementation of economic reforms of the 50s-90s. At the same time, a shortage of goods in the consumer market was created in its interests by fixing prices, which led to increased speculation and corruption. The equilibrium prices of the consumer market, which play an important role in optimising the supply structure, were excluded from the planning process of the economy as feedback for the planning. This doomed the rouble to defeat by the dollar. The reforms were aimed at giving more and more rights to enterprises to focus on profit, which intensified the chaos in public administration and led, ultimately, to the collapse of the country in 1991 with the restoration of capitalism and the transfer of management of the country's development to global management (Veduta,2019) **(1)**.

How are we to explain the aspiration of the nomenklatura to dismantle socialism?

It is necessary to note that Stalin eliminated the 'party maximum' **(see Notes)** in 1932 (Politburo Central Committee VKP (b), 1932) **(16)**. According to Academician E.S. Varga, the abolition of the party maximum contributed to the disintegration of Soviet society into layers with huge differences in income and the desire of the appointed Party nomenklatura for personal enrichment. Their example was followed by the bureaucracy and the lower strata, which was expressed in careerism, intrigues against competitors, and simple theft and corruption. The contradiction between the officially proclaimed communist morality and the real ideology of the ruling circles led to a widening gap between them and the working people and to the development of cynicism and careerism in society (Site: The Enemy of Capital, 2015) **(9).**

However, the steady transformation of a workers' state into a bureaucratic state following the abolition of the party maximum by Stalin was not a linear process. Also, there was an ideological struggle by those who, despite the creeping restoration of capitalism, continued to work for the benefit of practical implementation of communist ideals. During the Great Patriotic War, the authorities and the Party, led by Stalin, fully reflected the aspirations of the masses and brilliantly organised the victory. Evidently, from the discussions above, it is an undeniable historical truth that Stalin made an enormous contribution to the creation of the world's first socialist economy that managed to defeat fascism and become one of the centres of the bipolar world. Under his leadership, the USSR carried through its first industrialisation program, which eventually secured victory in the Second World War and which further enabled the post-war economic recovery.

Chapter III
Digital Projects of the Capitalist and Socialist Economy

A) Digital projects of the capitalist economy

Against the background of unprecedented progress in the field of cybernetics, AI, the current global economic crisis is the deepest in post-war peacetime. However, the introduction of digital technologies in the field of trade and financial services, workflow and controlling the people in the context of the ongoing economic chaos only reduces social productivity and leads civilisation to destruction for the sake of increasing the power of TNCs.

It should be noted that the material carrier of AI is a computer or a computing network that provides data exchange between computers and other computing devices to serve users. The goals of creating AI and algorithms for its functioning are determined by the interests of the dominant social strata and knowledge that generalises their experience of management.

TNCs striving to preserve capitalism and retain power set a course of "peaceful" destruction of production and a significant reduction in the population due to the introduction of AI in new speculative instruments such as "green" derivatives, cryptocurrencies, etc. The pandemic period has been used for the rapid development of AI to control people and the enrichment of the most advanced in the development of AI digital giants - Amazon, Apple, Microsoft, Facebook and Google, which threatens the absorption of all states.

All modern global projects from TNCs and the USA, such as "Inclusive Capitalism" (Veduta, 2021a **(17)**) and "New Green Deal" (Veduta, 2021b **(18)**), do not contain algorithms for overcoming the global crisis. They are aimed at preserving capitalism by constructing a better future for only a small group of TNC owners by worsening the lives of all other people and suppressing individualism, "who do not have the right to the future." Since the maintenance of TNCs in the conditions of an increasing level of automation and robotisation will require an ever smaller number of workers, this process will be accompanied by a significant reduction in the population. For this, the destruction of states and traditional values, material production using the "green" agenda, and the development of artificial intelligence and biotechnologies for the total control of modified people are supposed. The Chinese project "One Belt, One Road" implements the doctrine of liberalism for the expansion of China through the development of infrastructure in the countries of Eurasia and Africa and the subsequent flow of Chinese investment in these countries.

Since the crisis means the destruction of production and the deterioration of the life of the growing majority of citizens, the transition from the liberal economic model to the mobilisation management model becomes inevitable. There are two possible projects of a mobilisation management model for overcoming the current global crisis involving the use of AI:

- totalitarian management of people for the "peaceful" destruction of social production, impoverishment and death of the population with losses significantly exceeding those of the Second World War;
- effective management of the economy to improve the quality of life and comprehensive development of the individual.

There are naive ideas about the possibility of solving economic problems using "Big data" technologies of achieving economic planning using digital platforms based on algorithms for centralising and managing information without the influence of corrupt interests. The article by J. Thornhill notes the possibility of using state digital platforms for planning production. It quotes Jack Ma, founder of Alibaba, that Big Data will make the market smarter and will eventually build a planned economy (Thornhill, 2017 **(19)**).

However, "Big data" is a spontaneous set of indicators that will never solve the problem of proportional economic development. Without eliminating the causes of the global crisis, the expansion of "Big Data" only increases the workload of personnel and information chaos, leading to a stateless robotic society with mass unemployment and degradation of users of digitalisation's achievements that will be replaced by robots. (Standing, 2011) **(20)**. Digital slavery will be replaced by the digital primitive social order: (Kotkin, 2019) **(21),** (Brock, 2020), (Umair, 2021), (Couldry, 2019) and others.

Since within the framework of chaotically organised capitalism, there can be no effective management of the economy, in order to preserve capitalism, the introduction of AI to control people at the DNA level with their transformation into "happy" biorobots becomes inevitable. This process is served by the false narratives of the main ideologue, K. Schwab, with his 50 "great" like-minded people, about establishing a just and stable world if states "get the most out of technological potential and re-legitimise capitalism, making sure that the wealth of the few benefits a much larger part of society" (Schwab, 2022, p.79) **(22).**

Moreover, according to computer scientist Geoffrey Hinton, who left the post of Google Vice President due to ethical problems in the creation of AI, the world has approached the dangerous line of creating ingenious AI that surpasses human intelligence, which carries serious risks for humanity, in particular, creates opportunities for deadly autonomous weapons. (Khabidulina, 2023) **(23).**

In the concept of the fourth industrial revolution (Schwab, 2016 **(22)**) and the new trans-humanistic order (Schwab, 2020 **(23)**), Schwab replaces democracy with the dictatorship of TNCs, seeking to use the achievements of the digital revolution to establish complete digital control over humanity and its suppression, pushing civilisation to the "end of history."

Today, the words of the great cyberneticist Norbert Wiener are being confirmed: "Let us imagine that the second revolution is over. Then, the average person with average or even less ability will not be able to offer anything for sale that would be worth paying money for. There is only one way out - to build a society based on human values different from buying and selling. To build such a society will require a lot of preparation and a lot of struggles, which, under favourable circumstances, can be conducted on the ideological plane, and otherwise - who knows how?" (Wiener, 1958, p.79) **(24)**.

The scientific paradigm of Schwab's narratives is economic cybernetics. Its significance is growing for a progressively developing society. This paradigm underlies the creation of an cybernetic economy - automated system for managing the socialist economy in the interests of the people. This science originated in the USSR – the only country that had a history of purposefully attempting to use the processing power of computers to improve the quality of life for people. Not just different parts of society.

B) Digital projects of the socialist economy

Wiener's cybernetics was published in the USSR only in 1958 with a delay of 10 years. (Wienner, 1958). **(24).** In the same year, the Laboratory of Economics and Mathematical Methods in Moscow (later, the Central Economics and Mathematics Institute (CEMI)) and the Institute of Economics and Industrial Organization in Novosibirsk were created under the guidance of scientist-statistician V. Nemchinov. The source of inspiration for these two institutions was the econometric model of «input-output» by V. Leontiev, based on the use of statistics and mathematics. It was designed to make scenario forecasts, which had nothing to do with planning the economy.

Further, it would be another technocratic ideology of creating an automated control system (ACS), ignoring the laws of economic development, which was the basis for the development of the National Automated Control System (OGAS)at the Institute of Cybernetics in Kyiv. The Institute was founded in 1962 under the leadership of V. Glushkov. It was assumed that OGAS would include a state computer network connecting data collection centres located in all regions of the country and serving as the basis for the transition to optimal planning.

V. Glushkov and the Head of the CEMI N. Fedorenko wrote a remarkable article in 1964 about the reasons for the need to integrate computer technology into the management of the economy of the USSR (Glushkov, 1964) **(25).** They stated that depending on whether we manage to create OGAS for the economy or not, it will decide the fate of the country, and its victory in the Cold War will be decided accordingly. This article has set the goals to rigorously coordinate mutual efforts into the creation of OGAS, considering the huge advantages of a unified economic management system in the USSR in comparison with the United States, where each company pursues its own private interests.

This was well understood in the USA. In 1962, John Kennedy's adviser wrote a secret memorandum that "the Soviet decision to stake on cybernetics" would give the USSR a huge advantage with the use of ACS. If America continues to ignore cybernetics, the expert concluded, "we will be finished". (Pihorovich, 2019) **(26).**

However, in practice, as well as today, the narrowly selfish interests of the institutions were placed above those of the state. Glushkov, having no idea of what OGAS software should be, installed hardware that did not work. There were huge, ineffective costs for the introduction of huge computers in the businesses of the country. For this reason, his costly project was stopped to finance in 1970.

Today, all the developers of the digital economy are repeating Glushkov's mistake. Investments in the use of Big Data technology and AI are growing rapidly in TNCs, but their top managers do not yet understand what the benefits of them are. (Davenport, 2019) **(27)** The inefficiency of investments in technological progress is also forced to be acknowledged by Schwab, who notes that over the past 15 years, in advanced economies, there has been stagnation and, in some cases, even a regression in the level of productivity. (Schwab, 2022) **(22)**.

CEMI and the Institute of Novosibirsk focused more on the study of Western economic and mathematical models for writing scientific dissertations. The system of optimal functioning of the economy created by CEMI was based on hierarchical mathematical models of direct and dual tasks of linear and non-linear programming. These mathematical models and econometric modelling of inter-sectoral balance had nothing in common with the planning practice of GOSPLAN, which was forced to continue using the method of iterative manual planning.

Three institutions did not have enough time to develop a methodology and model for optimal planning because the narrow-minded interests of researchers were placed above the public interest. A lack of a scientific approach was reflected in the competition between these institutions for obtaining money to develop mathematical models for ACS, which affected the activities of the Main Computing Center of the country (MCC) of GOSPLAN, created in 1959 for the automation of system- planned calculations (ASPC).

In the absence of a dynamic model of intersectoral balance (MIB) coordinating the planned calculations of all industries and economic sectors to ensure its development in the desired direction, there was no interaction between sectoral ACS and ASPC. The MCC "stupidly" united branch computing systems and turned them into a body for analytical support of the Kosygin's reforms. While GOSPLAN asked to speed up the development of the ASPS, the sectoral ministries demanded more powers (Analytical Center, 2019) **(28)**.

In the absence of a dynamic MIB, the ASPC was reduced to a set of analytical tables created for different departments of GOSPLAN and the automated document management system "Document". Its task was to track the process of drawing up a plan but not to automate the actual planning calculations. Furthermore, the activity of the MCC was to be reduced to the unification of the networks of GOSPLAN with the computer systems of the republics, ministries and departments interacting in real-time. This gibberish was called by the Analytical Centre under the Government of Russia the creation of electronic government (Veduta,2019)

(29). The "Disease" of workflow automation instead of automating planned calculations, which ensures the movement of the economy in the direction of real income growth, is inherent today in all countries of the world. Today, this primitive approach develops the Analytical Centre for the Government of Russia, which calls this process the creation of an E-Government project (Analytical Center, 2019). **(28)**

If we return to the origins of the problem in the field of economic and mathematical modelling and automation of economic management, then we should recall the creation in 1962 in the capital of the third republic of Minsk of the Central Research Institute of Technical Management under the leadership of the scientist-cyberneticist, Nikolai Veduta. This institute introduced automated systems of economic management at a number of large enterprises. But Veduta's main success, who was a practitioner in the field of economic planning and the creation of the country's first automated control systems, consisted of the development of a dynamic MIB. The model is a system of mathematical algorithms describing the process of coordinating the orders of end consumers (government, households and exporters) and the capabilities of producers, including the procedure for adjusting initial assignments to achieve the input-output balance (Veduta, 2021) **(30)**.

In the course of calculations according to the model, the principles of optimising the structure of the final product are applied to increase the real solvency of the national currency, the effectiveness of the choice of new technological ways of production to maximise the rate of economic growth, while ensuring the fulfilment of macro-economic proportions and the condition of employment is ensured. The result of these calculations is the construction of production chains and the distribution of investments between industries in order to enter the trajectory of the growth in the quality of life.

The dynamic MIB is the only digital technology in the world that is able to "construct" the best future in the interests of all people (Veduta, 2016) **(31)**.

The main differences between Nikolai Veduta's cybernetic MIB and Vasily Leontiev's econometric MIB are as follows:

- λ *The method of building the model.* Economic cybernetics requires involving the reflection of objective economic laws when modelling inter-sectoral balance. Econometrics is based on statistics and mathematics.
- λ *In planning technology.* When constructing a cybernetic inter-sectoral balance, the method of successive approximations for calculating a plan is used, which implements the principles of

proportionality, production efficiency and optimisation of the consumption structure. This method always ensures the convergence and stability of solutions. The econometric model of inter-sectoral balance is based on scenario forecasts calculated on the basis of systems of equations, with forecast economic parameters obtained by methods of mathematical statistics. The solutions to the tasks of constructing intersectoral balance are unstable. The search for a solution is carried out by the selection method.

λ *Investments as a managing or predictive parameter.* Investments are the driving parameter of the plan in a cyber MIB. The allocation of investments is determined iteratively during the calculations of the plan. In econometrics, investments are a predictive parameter that does not interfere with lobbying for state support for the interests of those or other TNCs.

λ *Collecting information.* Cybernetic economy (an economic robot, or artificial intelligence in the economy, or ACS for managing the economy) is based on a cybernetic MIB that organises the flows of information on the output and costs of all types of products in physical terms with the aggregation of information into the nomenclature of MIB indicators and their subsequent disaggregation to bring the planned targets for the production of all types of products and by transactions online. The econometric MIB uses post-mortem information from statistical indicators compiled according to the UN National Accounting System and containing double count system statistics "posthumously" from the national accounting, containing repeated counts.

The scientist-philosopher V. Pikhorovich notes that Glushkov, unlike Veduta, had tremendous support from the country's leadership and was constantly busy promoting his idea. At the same time, N. Veduta, holding similar important and authoritative posts, was a lone enthusiast in developing the principles of automation and promoting his ideas. But he had a significant advantage over Glushkov since he was not only a professional cyberneticist but also a professionally serious and principled political economist. Veduta was the only cyberneticist among economists and the only economist among cyberneticians. Neither were among leading Soviet economists. (Pihorovich, 2014) **(32)**.

The time has come to unblock N. Veduta's cyber-planning to create a socialist economy.

Socialism is the only global cybernetic project that is presently capable of implementing a plan for social and cultural progress. Cybernetic economy or automation of economic management means the creation of an economic robot that coordinates the activities of all industries and sectors of the economy and all technical robots in order to increase the efficiency of management decisions in ensuring proportional development of the economy in the direction of improvement of the quality of life and comprehensive development of the individual.

Lenin once said that socialism is Soviet power plus the electrification of the whole country. Today, this slogan can be paraphrased as "socialism is democracy plus cybernetic economy." The introduction of cybernetic economy that automates managerial work will mean the second industrial (cybernetic) revolution, which will ensure the irrevocable transition from capitalism to socialism.

Conclusions

Since the 16th century, the economic policy of states has been characterised by the cyclical nature of "mercantilism - war - liberalism....". In the 20th century, with the coming to power of TNCs, this was transformed into the cyclicality of "inflation - war - financial stabilisation....". At the beginning of the 20th century, when the dominance of TNCs was established, inflation, the world monetary system based on the use of key reserve currencies, and the world market for loan capital were added to the instruments of economic policy of the 16th - 19th centuries. These financial instruments, using flows of fictitious capital, redistribute produced income and assets in favour of TNCs, increasing technological and social inequality in the world. After the collapse of the USSR in 1991, a unipolar system was established, plunging the world into a deepening global crisis.

2. Speculative games end with protectionism and preparations for a new military solution to the unfolding crisis. With the coming to power of Trump in the United States in 2017, the world entered another phase of pre-war mercantilism, manifested in a sharp increase in trade and sanctions wars and a new arms race. Considering the nuclear potential of developing countries and therefore trying to avoid direct military conflict, TNCs added to their instruments the achievements of the digital revolution.

3. The pandemic has revealed to almost everyone the goals of TNCs seeking to use the possibilities of the digital revolution and biotechnology to preserve capitalism by establishing total control over human behaviour, bringing the "end of human history" closer.

4. The only alternative to capitalism is socialism. The first attempt to organise a non-capitalist, proportionally developing economy in the direction of a prosperous future was made by the USSR. The historical analysis of the development of the economic policy of the USSR from war communism to the NEP and then to the course of industrialisation shows how the country, gradually accumulating a balanced experience in economic planning, moved to use the method of successive approximations (iterations) to the drawing up of plans. Its most important principles are consideration of feedback in the process of coordinating planned calculations "input-output" and rolling planning (adjustment of planned calculations online). Thanks to this, in essence, cybernetic planning of the economy, the USSR won the Second World War and became the power of the bipolar world, determining the vector of global development.

5. Reasons for the defeat of the USSR in the US Cold War:

- the elimination of the party maximum in the early 1930s contributed to the disintegration of Soviet society into social strata with a huge difference in income and the desire of the appointed Party nomenklatura for personal enrichment, the flourishing of cynicism, careerism and corruption in society
- the objective and subjective difficulties of the country, which was the first country in the world to implement the planning of the national economy by the method of successive approximations, to develop a planning model that allows moving from manual planning focused on industrialisation to cybernetic (automated) planning focused on the growth of real incomes of citizens.
- the adoption of the theory of commodity production under socialism in 1956 as the official doctrine for reforming the economy by granting enterprises more and more independence and, thus, restoring the capitalist economy in the interests of the Party nomenklatura;

- underestimation of the dominant role of economic cybernetics in the development of the theory and practice of economic planning for the transition from manual to automated planning in order to improve the efficiency of managerial decisions in ensuring the growth of real incomes of citizens.
- continuation of the hitherto course of industrialisation, which meant disproportionate development and implementation of economic reforms, intensifying economic chaos, and also the shadow market arising from the fixation of prices in the consumer market, led the country that had carried out the first experiment in planning a socialist economy into a deep economic crisis that ended with the collapse of the country in 1991.

6. In the context of a pandemic, digital technologies have been added to the financial instruments of TNCs in the field of trade and financial services, workflow and AI in order to control people. Realising the need to reduce risks from coordinating production relationships through international trade, Western experts place hope on "Big Data" technology. It, in their opinion, will lead the world to use economic planning with the help of algorithms and without the corruption that emerged in the USSR. Such a statement testifies to the lack of understanding by Western experts of the essence of cyber planning in the USSR and, therefore, the impossibility of creating algorithms that would provide a way out of the global crisis.

7. The key to finding a way out of the global crisis should be sought in the alternative experience of planning the socialist economy of the USSR. Its improvement assumed the transition from manual to automated control system (ACS), ensuring proportional development of the economy in the direction of the growth of the real incomes of citizens. To create an cybernetic economy - ACS (economic robot), knowledge of economic cybernetics, the science of information processes in social production, was required, allowing for the development of algorithms for coordinating planned "input-output" calculations to ensure the movement of the economy in the desired direction, i.e., cyber planning.

8. It was recognised in the USSR and the USA that if the USSR had time to create a State ACS (OGAS) for the economy, then today, the world would be completely different, moving towards a prosperous future. Difficulties in developing a dynamic MIB and the narrowly selfish interests of the institutions responsible for the implementation of ACS led to their competition for receiving money for research unrelated to improving the planning of a socialist economy.

9. Thanks to the knowledge of Marx's Capital and the experience of management at all levels of economic management in the USSR, the Soviet cybernetic scientist Nikolay Veduta developed a dynamic MIB. His model is the only digital technology in the world that constructs and directs the development of the economy towards a prosperous future.

10. Today, the cybernetic approach to economic planning is blocked all over the world. At the same time, huge state funds are spent for the narrowly selfish interests of digital giants who are adversely leading the world into "dark times". The time has come to unblock cybernetic planning for the implementation of an economic robot that coordinates the activities of all industries and sectors of the economy towards a prosperous future. Its implementation will mean a management (cybernetic) revolution in the economy that will significantly increase the efficiency of state (global) management. Just as the introduction of machines at one time meant the first industrial revolution, affirming capitalism, so the introduction of the cybernetic economy (economic robot) will mean the second industrial revolution, affirming socialism without the possibility of capitalist restoration.

References

(1) Veduta Elena (2019) Why USSR lost the economic war, and the West will lose now. Regnum agency.
RETRIEVED FROM:
https://regnum.ru/news/economy/2606859.html
(Publication date: 07.04.19).

(2) Marx Karl (1951). Capital, volume 1, chapter 13. M.: "Gospolitizdat", 1951.

(3) Veduta EN (2023) Strategy and Economic Policy of the State. Publisher: NITs INFRA-M, 2023.

(4) Pesenti A.(1976) Essays on Political Economy of Capitalism. Volume I. M.: Publisher: Progress, 1976.

(5) Marx K. (1951) Capital, volume 3, chapter 30. M.: "Gospolitizdat", 1951.

(6) The White House. (2018) Strategy for National Cyber Security. SEPTEMBER 2018.
RETRIEVED FROM:
https://trumpwhitehouse.archives.gov/wp-content/uploads/2018/09/National-Cyber-Strategy.pdf
(Date visited: 23.07.21).

(7) Lutsenko AV (2018) K. Marx and A. Bogdanov about the Revolution in Russia. Bulletin of Tomsk State University. History.2018, №52.
RETRIEVED FROM:https://cyberleninka.ru/article/n/k-marks-i-a-bogdanov-o-revolyutsii-v-rossii/viewer

(8) Administration of the affairs of the Council of People's Commissars of the USSR (1944) Collection of legalizations and orders of the government for 1921. Decree of the Council of People's Commissars № 106. Regulations on the State General Planning Commission. M.:1944, p.161-162. RETRIEVED FROM: https://istmat.org/node/45925

(9) Site: The enemy of capital (2015) Stalin Inequality. RETRIEVED FROM: https://1917.com/History/I-II/rmZH0i30fEkZSDSDxKo7uOw3aNg.html

(10) Elmeev VYa, Ovsyannikov VG (1999) Applied Sociology. Essays on methodology. Publishing house of St. Petersburg State University, 1999. RETRIEVED FROM: http://read.newlibrary.ru/read/elmeev_v_ja__ovsjannikov_v_g_/page0/prikladnaja_sociologija__ocherki_metodologii.html (Date visited: 23.07.21).

(11) Stalin JV(1929) Collected works of Stalin JV (1879–1953). Volume 12, p.11. Pravda No. 309, December 29, 1929. M.: Marx Engels Lenin Institute under the Central Committee of the All-Union Communist Party of Bolsheviks - 13 volumes (from 1946 to 1952). RETRIEVED FROM: https://thelib.ru/books/stalin_iosif_vissarionovich/tom_12-read-11.html (Date visited: 23.07.21).

(12) Koen S. (1988) Bukharin. Political Biography 1888-1938. M.: Progress,1988.

(13) Autonomov V.S., Ananjin O.I., Makasheva N.A. (2000) History of Economic Studies. Economic Discussions 1920-s on the Nature of Planned Economy. M.: INFRA-M, 2000.
RETRIEVED FROM:
https://www.gumer.info/bibliotek_Buks/Econom/avton/.

(14) Barr R. (1995) Political Economy. M.: International Relations, 1995

(15) A Logvinov. Artels and consumer cooperation under Stalin's rule. Proza.ru Krasnoyarsk, December, 2021
RETRIEVED FROM: https://proza.ru/2021/12/29/1277

(16) Politburo Central Committee VKP (b). (1932) Protocol № 87 sessions of the Politburo Central Committee VKP (b) from 8 February 1932. On the rates for communist business executives and engineering staff. Annex No. 2 to paragraph 9 of the PB No. 87 dated 8.II.1932Attachment № 2 k p. 9 пр. РВ № 87.
RETRIEVED FROM: https://istmat.org/node/54451 (Date visited: 23.07.21).

Site: The enemy of capital. (2015) Stalin Inequality. RETRIEVED FROM: http://www.1917.com/History/I-II/rmZH0i30fEkZSDSDxKo7uOw3aNg.html (Date visited: 23.07.21).

(17) Veduta EN (2021a) Manifesto of inclusive capitalism: wolves will remain full, but what about the sheep? 18.01.2021 Regnum agency.
RETRIEVED FROM:
https://regnum.ru/news/3165745.html (Date visited: 23.07.21).

(18) Veduta EN (2021b). The new "green" course is designed to completely destroy our economy. Business online newspaper "Business Online". 26.05.2021
RETRIEVED FROM: https://www.business-gazeta.ru/article/510656 (Date visited: 23.07.21).

(19) Thornhill J. (2017) The Big Data revolution can revive the planned economy. Financial Times
RETRIEVED FROM:
https://www.ft.com/content/6250e4ec-8e68-11e7-9084-d0c17942ba93 (Date visited: 23.07.21).

(20) Standing G. (2011) The Precariat: The New Dangerous Class. A&C Black. 2011

(21) Kotkin J. (2019) America's Drift toward Feudalism. American Affairs. Volume III, Number 4 (Winter 2019): 96–107
RETRIEVED FROM:
https://americanaffairsjournal.org/2019/11/americas-drift-toward-feudalism/

Haque U. (2020) Our Civilization Needs a Great Transformation. We Need Three Decades of Revolutions. But Are We Capable of It? 25.07.20. RETRIEVED FROM: https://eand.co/our-civilization-needs-a-great-transformation-d2da2c84e34e (Date visited: 23.07.21).

Couldry N. and Ulises A. Megias (2019) The Costs of Connection. How Data Is Colonizing Human Life and Appropriating It for Capitalism. Series: Culture and Economic Life. Stanford University Press, 2019.

(22) Schwab K. and Malleret T (2022). The Great Narranive For a Better Future. World Economic Forum, 2022, p.79).

(23) Khabidulina E. The "Godfather" of Artificial Intelligence Left Google and Announced the Dangers of AI. Editorial Forbes. 02.05.2023.
RETRIEVED FROM:
https://www.forbes.ru/tekhnologii/488692-krestnyj-otec-iskusstvennogo-intellekta-usel-iz-google-i-zaavil-ob-opasnosti-ii

(24) Wiener N. (1958) Cybernetics, or Control and Communication in an Animal and Machine. M.: Soviet Radio, 1958.

(25) Glushkov V., Fedorenko N. (1964) Problems of widespread introduction of computer technology in the national economy. Questions of Economics, N 7 1964.

RETRIEVED FROM: http://v-v-glushkova.narod.ru/index/0-21

(26) Pihorovich V. (2019) Essays on the history of cybernetics in the USSR, M.: Lenand, 2019.

RETRIEVED FROM: https://www.rulit.me/books/ocherki-istorii-kibernetiki-v-sssr-read-730842-1.html

(27) Davenport T (2019). Why businesses can't benefit from big data. Vedomosty, 29.07.2019) https://www.vedomosti.ru/management/articles/2019/07/28/807480-bolshih-dannih.

(28) Analytical Center under the Government of the Russian Federation. (2019) Pioneers of digitalization. 1959/2019

RETRIEVED FROM: https://ac.gov.ru/uploads/pdf/About._Documents._01/60_let_web.pdf

(29) Veduta E., Evtushenko S., Haritonov Ju (2019) Will politicians be able to control the economy? Regnum agency, 12.08.2019

RETRIEVED FROM: https://regnum.ru/article/2687986

(30) Veduta N. (2021) Digitalization of economic planning. Cybernetic approach Gaudeamus, 2021.

(31) Veduta E. (2016) Interindustry-intersectoral balance. The mechanism of strategic planning of the economy. Akademproekt, 2016.

(32) Pihorovich V. (2014) The concept of socially effective economy of Veduta N. 02.10.2014.
RETRIEVED FROM:
http://spinoza.in/theory/kontseptsiya-sotsial-no-effektivnoj-e-konomiki-n-i-veduty-chast-1.html (date visited: 23.05.19).

Appendix

**A note on Party maximum
(From Wikipedia and the Internet)**

Party maximum or 'Partmaximum' (Russian: Партмаксимум) was a limit on the salary of a member of the Communist Party of the Soviet Union, a maximum wage. The landmark idea came from the Paris Commune of 1871. It was introduced in the Soviet Union in 1920 by a decree of the All-Russian Central Executive Committee (ВЦИК) for all communists that held executive positions in Party, industry, government and Soviet trade unions.

According to partmaximum, the salary of the abovementioned was not to exceed that of a highly qualified industrial worker. If a communist had other incomes, e.g., honoraria or royalties, he had to transfer a specified percentage from the amount above the partmaximum into the Party funds.

Partmaximum was withdrawn by a resolution of the Politburo of February 8, 1932. The adopted resolution was signed by V Molotov, *Chairman of the Council of People's Commissars of the USSR* and I Stalin, *Secretary of the Central Committee* of\ the CPSU.

www.ingramcontent.com/pod-product-compliance
Lightning Source LLC
Chambersburg PA
CBHW071727020426
42333CB00017B/2425